the native american *look book*

kwakiutl

zuni

pomo

art and activities from The Brooklyn Museum

the native american *look book*

The Brooklyn Museum

Missy Sullivan, Deborah Schwartz, Dawn Weiss,
and Barbara Zaffran

The New Press, New York

Library of Congress Cataloging-in-Publication Data
Schwartz, Deborah.

The Native American look book: art and activities from the Brooklyn Museum / written by Deborah Schwartz, Missy Sullivan, Dawn Weiss, and Barbara Zaffran.

p.   cm.
"Based upon an original program created by Dorothea Basile."
Includes bibliographical references.
Summary: Introduces Native American art and culture by examining a Kwakiutl whale mask, a Zuni water jar, and a Pomo basket at the Brooklyn Museum.
ISBN 1-56584-022-4 (hardcover)
1. Indian art—North America—Juvenile literature. 2. Kwakiutl wood-carving—Juvenile literature. 3. Zuni pottery—Juvenile literature. 4. Pomo baskets—Juvenile literature. [1. Indian art—North America. 2. Indians of North America—Social life and customs.
3. Art appreciation.] I. Weiss, Dawn. II. Zaffran, Barbara. III. Brooklyn Museum. IV. Title.
E98.A7S93
1996
730'.089'979—dc20
95-36245
CIP
AC

Published in the United States by The New Press, New York
Distributed by W. W. Norton & Company, Inc., New York

Established in 1990 as a major alternative to the large, commercial publishing houses, The New Press is a full-scale nonprofit American book publisher outside of the university presses. The Press is operated editorially in the public interest, rather than for private gain; it is committed to publishing in innovative ways works of educational, cultural, and community value that, despite their intellectual merits, might not normally be commercially viable. The New Press's editorial offices are located at the City University of New York.

Book design by
Salsgiver Coveney Associates

Production management by
Kim Waymer

Printed in the United States of America

96 97 98 99 9 8 7 6 5 4 3 2 1

Written by Missy Sullivan, Deborah Schwartz, Dawn Weiss, and Barbara Zaffran
Based upon an original program created by Dorothea Basile
Project Director: Deborah Schwartz
Project Advisers: Sonnet Takahisa, Diana Fane, Ira Jacknis, and Carol Cornelius

contents

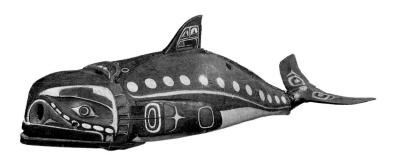

kwakiutl

zuni

pomo

foreword and acknowledgments

Since early in this century, The Brooklyn Museum has played a significant role in presenting and interpreting American Indian art. By 1912, Stewart Culin, the curator of the Department of Ethnology, had acquired more than nine thousand Indian artifacts. In 1991, The Brooklyn Museum presented an extraordinary exhibition called *Objects of Myth and Memory: American Indian Art at The Brooklyn Museum*. The exhibition introduced the objects Culin collected as well as some of the issues raised by historic and contemporary collecting of Native American works of art. It was the culmination of seven years of research and planning led by Diana Fane, the curator responsible for the Museum's Native American art collection, who worked with colleagues and consultants across the country. At the same time, the Museum mounted an exhibition entitled *A Dialogue with Tradition*, which highlighted the work of contemporary Native American artists and explored the continuation of Native American artistic traditions.

The programs developed in conjunction with these two exhibitions enabled the Museum's Education Division staff to explore many different ways in which children and adults can appreciate and learn about Native American art. Indeed, for years The Brooklyn Museum's educators have been developing inventive teaching techniques to help people look carefully at works of art. On almost any visit to the Museum you will encounter children and adults attending talks, listening to storytelling programs, making art, and participating in programs with working artists.

The authors worked closely with the staff to present a variety of these ideas in a book. We hope that adults and children will be able to share at home some of these ways of looking at and thinking about art. We also urge you to visit The Brooklyn Museum, other museums, and Native American cultural centers across the land so that you can experience the pleasures of looking at works of art in person.

Many people contributed to the ideas and production of this book.

Thanks especially go to the authors, Missy Sullivan, Dawn Weiss, and Barbara Zaffran, and to Salsgiver Coveney Associates for the beautiful design. I also wish to acknowledge the staff at The New Press: André Schiffrin, Ellen Reeves, Hall Smyth, David Sternbach, Jessica Blatt, and Dawn Davis, for their extraordinary enthusiasm and support of the Museum and in particular for this book. From The Brooklyn Museum staff, our special thanks go to Sonnet Takahisa for helping to conceptualize this project in the early stages. Thanks also go to Museum staff Jennifer Baron, Dorothea Basile, Diana Fane, Elaine Koss, Judith Ostrowitz, Erika Sanger, and Rena Zurofsky. Others who have helped advise include the specialists Ira Jacknis and Carol Cornelius. With admiration and respect I express thanks to artists Susan Billy, Randy Nahohai, and Richard Hunt, without whom this book would not have been possible. Finally, I wish to thank Deborah Schwartz for the vision and commitment that made the production of this book possible.

ROBERT T. BUCK
Director, The Brooklyn Museum

introduction

This is a book about looking carefully at three works of art made by Native American Indians. By looking closely, you can learn about the materials and processes used to make them, the functions they serve, and the importance they have to the people who use them.

You will also find out about three contemporary Native American artists, whose work has been inspired by their tribes' artistic traditions. Each of them has developed a special dialogue between past and present.

We have designed this book for children and adults to use together. After looking, reading, and trying some of the activities, you will have learned some new ways to look at and enjoy works of art. You may want to use some of the ideas presented here the next time you explore a museum. At the end of this book we have provided some suggestions for other books to read and places to visit to learn more about Native American art and culture.

No single book will have all the answers to your questions. It is our hope that this one will help you appreciate the process of looking at art, help you discover some interesting things about Native American art and culture, and inspire you to want to learn more and to look at more works of art. Remember, look carefully—the more you look, the more you will see.

kwakiutl

Whale Mask (Kwakiutl)

The mask is 24 inches high, 68 inches long, and 28 ¼ inches wide. It is made of cedar wood, hide (animal skin), cotton cord, leather, nails, and pigment (color). The Brooklyn Museum purchased the mask in 1908.

looking at a kwakiutl whale mask

look for the designs on the mask

Do you think that real whales have designs such as these? Can you see anything that you recognize in the shapes? (*Hint: Do the white dots along its back look like bubbles? Why would they be near the blowhole?*) Look for the parts of this whale mask that might move. During a winter dance ceremony, the movable parts help the dancer tell his story. Which parts move?

Imagine that you live on the Northwest Coast of North America. It's winter, cold and rainy, so you're indoors a lot. Your pantry is full and you don't need to worry about getting food for dinner. Your family and friends get together for costume shows with special dances. These dances tell stories, teach ancient beliefs, and express community values.

For the Kwakiutl people of the Northwest Coast, lavish ceremonial and social gatherings like these are an important part of tribal culture. A Kwakiutl carver made this whale mask for a dancer to wear during such an event.

Imagine putting this mask on your head and pretending to be a whale.

look at the whale mask

and read the description of it on the opposite page. Pay special attention to its size and the materials from which it is made. How is this mask different from masks you have worn? Have you ever seen a mask this big? What would it feel like to touch? Do you think it is heavy? How would it feel to dance with this mask on your head and back?

look for the whale's flukes

(*the pointy tips of its tail*). Can you find its pectoral (*side*) fins? Dorsal (*top*) fin? What about the whale's blowhole, which it uses to breathe, on top of its head? Can you see a second face carved there? Does a real whale have two faces? Why might the carver have given the whale a second face? (*Think about how you move around when you dance.*)

a kwakiutl carver *at work*

① The carver chooses the tree that best suits the form of the mask he has in mind. The forests of the Northwest Coast provide lots of red cedar wood, which is soft-grained and easy to split. Kwakiutl carvers also like to work with yellow cedar and alder.

② Then the carver chops down the tree. He removes the outer bark and sapwood and splits the log to the size he wants.

③ He uses tools to cut and shape the wood into a mask, working on both the front and the back. Early carvers used tools made out of stone, antler, bone, and wood. Today, carvers are more likely to use metal tools.

④ He then drills holes on the sides for a thong or band to hold the mask in place.

⑤ Next he paints the mask to enhance or embellish the carved forms. Traditional Kwakiutl color choices are dark red, black, white, and occasionally dark green. Before paints could be bought in a store, carvers made them out of burnt clam shells, clay, mud, charcoal, or other natural materials. Carvers ground these materials together with salmon eggs, in small stone dishes, to provide an oily base.

questions and answers about kwakiutl culture

Where do the Kwakiutl live?

For centuries, the Kwakiutl people have lived along the Northwest Coast of North America, from the shores of what we now call Washington State up to the lower part of Alaska. (See map p. 48)

How has their environment affected their culture?

Like many other tribes along the Northwest Coast, the Kwakiutl relied on the ocean. They traveled by sea in large, elaborate canoes to hunt, fish, trade, visit neighbors, or wage war. The Pacific Ocean was rich with fish and sea mammals and so the Kwakiutl didn't have to worry about finding food. Their great skill as fishermen enabled them to stock up for the winter and spend those months carving, weaving, and dancing instead of hunting. The dense forests of the region provided plenty of wood for Kwakiutl artists to carve, and roots and bark for them to weave.

When do the Kwakiutl wear masks?

Masks are worn by dancers during social and ceremonial gatherings called potlatches.

What is a potlatch?

A potlatch is a tribal gathering held to mark important family occasions, such as the naming of a child, the building of a house, the raising of a totem pole, a marriage, or a death. In Chinook, a language developed by traders, potlatch means "to give." A typical potlatch includes feasting, family dances, elaborate dramas, and ritual gift-giving. The host family publicly claims certain stories, and shows its wealth and status by giving away some of its property. The more it gives, the more status it passes on to future generations of the family.

Northwest Coast landscape

questions and answers about kwakiutl culture

Who uses a whale mask?
One Kwakiutl family tells a special story, the Siwidi legend. You can read it on page 13. This means that they have the right to use a whale mask (or masks of any other animals in the Siwidi legend). This family may show the masks and dance them during a potlatch festival.

Why is the whale important to the Kwakiutl people?
Because the Kwakiutl people are so oriented to the sea, they have learned to respect all of its creatures, especially the awesome whale. The whale plays many important roles in Kwakiutl mythology. A whale mask may appear in a potlatch as a chief's treasure.

Family in front of totem poles, Massel, Queen Charlotte Island

Is this a killer whale mask?
The whale mask we have been looking at represents a baleen whale, not a killer whale. Unlike the killer whale, the baleen has no teeth. Instead of hunting for food, it just opens its mouth and swallows small crustaceans. They also look a little different: a baleen has a short, curved dorsal fin, and long pectoral fins, while a killer whale has a tall dorsal fin.

Do the Kwakiutl also make totem poles?
Yes, they do. Totem poles are made from tall trees that families have carved from top to bottom with images of animals that are important to them. If a family ancestor had a special experience with a bear, for example, a legend arose from this, and the bear became the family symbol and was carved on the totem pole.

What other things do the Kwakiutl carve?
Kwakiutl artists are well known for their distinctive and elaborate carving, which they apply to everything from boxes, rattles, and whistles to much larger items like canoes and house fronts.

Do both men and women carve?
In traditional Kwakiutl culture, only men took on the jobs of hunting, fishing, woodworking, carving, and painting. Women's jobs included gathering and cooking food, housekeeping, and weaving blankets, clothing, baskets, and fishing nets.

Do the Kwakiutl still make masks today?
Yes, they still weave and dance and hold potlatch ceremonies on special occasions. Richard Hunt is a Kwakiutl carver who makes masks, totem poles, and other traditional objects. You can see a photograph of him and his artwork on page 16.

the legend of siwidi

Adapted from "Kwakiutl Texts, Second Series," *Publications of the Jesup North Pacific Expedition,* by Frank Boaz and George Hunt, 1906.

Whales play an important part in Kwakiutl mythology. Although the whale mask we have been looking at represents a baleen whale, stories about killer whales are more plentiful in Kwakiutl culture because they are considered more powerful. This tale includes a killer whale. It can only be told (and its masks can only be worn) by the Kwakiutl family that holds the privilege of reenacting this legend in a potlatch ceremony.

Once there was a boy named Siwidi who was lazy and slept all the time. His father scolded him and told him that he should be more like his older brother. Siwidi was very sad and went to sit by the lake, where he noticed something moving. After a while, an octopus rose from the water, surrounded him with its tentacles, and dragged him down. Siwidi soon found himself in the magnificent house of the chief of the undersea kingdom.

Siwidi visited this fabulous home for a short time, and then the chief of the undersea world ordered two killer whales to take the boy on an expedition to visit all of the other undersea tribes. During his travels he developed supernatural powers. Four years later, when Siwidi returned from this journey, it seemed to him that he had only been away four days.

The chief gave Siwidi his house and a new name to celebrate his newfound powers. His new name was Born-to-Be-Head-of-the-World. After the celebrations, Siwidi took his new house and floated up to the top of the lake, right near his old home. His family and all the other members of the tribe tried to catch him, but they couldn't because Siwidi kept changing from one sea creature to another. At one moment he was a sculpin fish, and then in an instant he became a killer whale. Finally, he became a man again and told the tribe to create a place for his magical house. Born-to-Be-Head-of-the-World also brought with him permission to perform a masked dance about his adventure. He held a winter dance—a potlatch—for his people.

thinking about kwakiutl masks

design

Thunderbird
Transformation Mask (Kwakiutl)
When closed, this mask shows a thunderbird head in profile. Can you see where the curved beak would be?

Carved and Painted Box
This panel from a carved box may be Kwakiutl, or it may have been made by another Northwest Coast tribe.

Whale Mask details
dorsal (top) fin
pectoral (side) fin
tail

When you first look at designs, they may just seem like shapes. But the more carefully you look, the more you may see things you recognize. Northwest Coast Indian artists often use the symbols and designs seen on these objects.

Look at the designs on the thunderbird mask. How many different faces and/or creatures do you see? Can you find a shape that looks like a hand? an eye? a tongue? a beak? teeth?

Now look at the shapes on the box panel, the whale mask, and the thunderbird. Can you find any that look alike? Why do you think artists used such similar shapes?

animals

Northwest Coast tribal people place a lot of importance on animals. Families identify themselves on their totem poles with animals, including bears, wolves, beavers, frogs, ravens, thunderbirds, and whales. Northwest Coast myths are filled with animals and sea creatures with supernatural powers. Dancers tell tribal stories wearing animal masks.

Think about how animals can symbolize certain qualities (like the courageous lion or the cunning fox). Think about any animals that have special meanings for you.

Transformation

Have you ever dreamed of turning into another being? That would be a magical process, of course. If you turned into a whale, how would you change? What would you be like? How would you act?

If you were trying to impress your friends, what kind of mask would you wear?

How can a mask encourage a magical transformation? Think about how some aspects of the whale mask make it seem very real, like the moving parts and the fact that it is so big and heavy. Then consider how other aspects, like the extra face and the special designs, might make it different (perhaps more magical) than a real whale.

For Northwest Coast Indians, birds are important mythological figures. Some have supernatural powers, such as the thunderbird. Eagles and ravens also appear often as masks, on totem poles, and on other carved objects.

Wolf Clan Helmet
This helmet was made by an artist in the Haida tribe, a people who live on the Northwest Coast near the Kwakiutl. The wolf head on top of this helmet identified its wearer as a member of the wolf clan.

15

keeping the tradition *alive*

Richard Hunt carving a totem pole

I was taught by my father, Henry Hunt, and followed the potlatch all my life. When I started carving it was more to make money. As I got older I started to realize that what I carved actually belonged to my people. Whenever I carve something like the killer whale mask I feel I am reclaiming the rights to this dance for the Kwakiutl people and when I dance the killer whale mask I feel I am taking on the spirit of the killer whale. Our elders say that the killer whale possesses the spirits of our great chiefs.

Richard Hunt

Whale mask by Richard Hunt

Richard Hunt
was born in 1951 on Cormorant Island, near Vancouver Island, Canada. When he was thirteen, he learned the art of carving from his father. He has made many traditional items, such as masks, rattles, bowls, house posts, grave markers, and totem poles. He has even made a full-size whaling canoe. He also paints, makes prints, engraves jewelry, and designs clothing. In addition, he is experienced in the rituals and dances of Kwakiutl culture. For many years he was the chief carver at the British Columbia Provincial Museum. He now lives in Victoria, Canada. Richard's Indian name is Gwe-la-yo-gwe-la-gya-les, which means "a man who travels around the world giving."

How does Richard Hunt help keep the Kwakiutl mask-making tradition alive?
Compare his mask to the one we have been looking at. At first glance, they look fairly similar. What looks the same? What looks different? Compare the fins, the tail, the shape, the head, the mouth, and the designs.

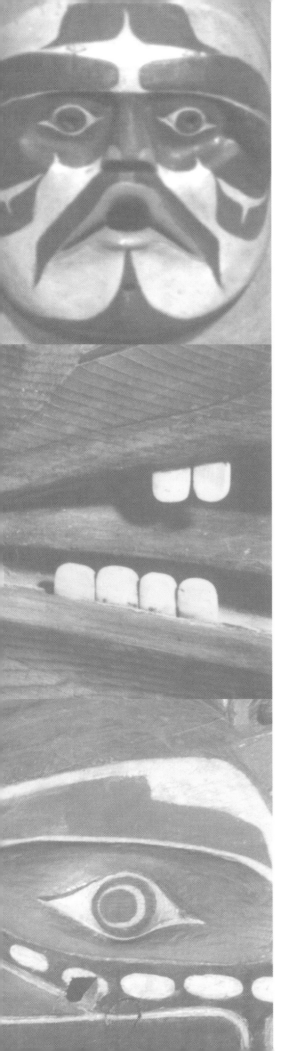

doing it for yourself

getting symbol savvy

Imagine that you're a Kwakiutl storyteller who uses animals to tell tales about people. To help you get across your characters' special qualities, you've created a list of animal symbols. Which creatures would you choose to symbolize people who were

sly?   evil?

　　meek?   fast?

courageous?   greedy?

　　stubborn?   humorous?

slow?   vain?

design your own mask

If you had to choose one creature to be your own personal symbol, what would it be? Why? What do you have in common?

After you've decided what animal you might like to be, draw designs to create your own mask. Try to fill in the space the way a Kwakiutl artist might. You may want to color it with Kwakiutl colors: black, red, dark green, and white.

The pot on the right is 11 inches high, and 13 ¾ inches around. The pot on the left is 12 inches high and 14 ½ inches around. Both pots are made out of clay and slip (a wet mixture of clay and water). They were purchased by Stewart Culin for The Brooklyn Museum in 1904.

zuni

looking at zuni water jars

Almost one hundred years ago, when these water jars were made in the deserts of the southwestern United States, the Zuni people didn't have faucets and running water. Back then, they used clay jars like these to carry water from the well or the river and to store it in their houses.

think about the size of the jars

Are they a good size and shape for carrying? How heavy would they be if they were filled with water? (Think of the weight of a gallon of milk or water at the grocery store.) How easy would they be to use if they were any bigger? Would they be useful if they were any smaller? How long do you think the water lasted before a family had to go get more?

look at the shape of the jars

Notice especially how the top (the lip) curves in and up from the lower part (the body). If you lived in the desert before refrigerators were invented, would this shape help keep your water shaded and cool? Why? Would it help keep bugs and dust and other things from falling into your water? Would it make pouring easy?

notice how the jars are decorated

How many colors do you see on the surface of each pot? What color were the pots before they were painted? (Look at the edge, where the paint has worn away. Then think of what the pots are made of.)

now look at the designs

Do you recognize any of the animals? (Think about which ones have antlers.) What other shapes do you see? Which parts of the design seem to go all the way around the pot? Many of the designs, even the geometric shapes, have meaning for the Zuni people. The geometric shapes on the pot to the left are said to show rain falling from a summer storm. This design is called "the rainbird." Can you see a part that looks like a tail? or feathers? You'll have to use your imagination on this one.

A Zuni woman carrying a pot on her head.

a zuni potter *at work*

How are clay pots made?

Have you ever worked with clay? For the Zuni, making water jars was a necessary chore that they turned into an art form.

Paint Mortar with Pestles

Zuni potters traditionally used this tool, called a mortar and pestle, to grind up pigments, or colors, into a dry powder. Pigments came from plants, berries, and other natural sources. Once ground, the pigments were mixed with a liquid to make paints.

Polishing Stones

These stones are rubbed on the surface of the clay pot to smooth it before it is put in the oven.

①

First the clay has to be collected and prepared. According to Zuni tradition, the gatherers must not talk while digging up the clay. If they do, it is said, the clay pot will crack while being baked.

②

The artist rolls the clay into coils, which he or she connects by smoothing them together with broken pieces of another pot. As the pot is shaped, the artist imagines the design on the finished pot, using birds, deer, clouds, or rain for inspiration.

③

The artist places a piece of bread in each pot before firing so that the spirit of the pot may be fed by the spirit of the bread.

④

In order to fire the pots, the potter makes an oven of dried sheep and goat manure. The manure surrounds and covers the pots. The artist builds a structure around the pots. Then more sheep and goat dung is piled around the structure and burnt as fuel.

questions and answers about zuni culture

The potters who made the Museum's water jars lived in a pueblo like this one. Do you see any trees, grass, or water? The Zuni made almost everything from their homes to their jars out of the earth around them.

Where do the Zuni live?

They live in the southwestern United States, in what is now Arizona and New Mexico. The climate there is desertlike (hot and dry), and water is a precious resource. The Zuni live in pueblos, or small communities. The word "pueblo" derives from the Spanish word for "village." At the time these pots were made, Zuni pueblos were made up of closely-spaced adobe (earthen) houses.

What is Zuni pottery used for?

For hundreds of years, the Zuni have used pottery to hold water, food, and other things. Sometimes they use pots in religious ceremonies. Now that they can get water from the faucet or buy it at the store, the Zuni don't have to make water jars anymore. But they do. Today, a Zuni family might also use jars like these to store important religious objects.

Is all Zuni pottery decorated?

No. Cookware is generally left unpainted.

What are the symbols on their pottery?

Some symbols are wishes for good luck. Others tell stories. Few symbols are just for decoration, although some have meanings that have been lost over time. Because Zuni land is so dry and hot, pottery makers often paint symbols of rain onto their work. They may "fill in" painted designs with thin, slanting lines (called hatching) to represent falling rain. They also paint dragonflies, tadpoles, frogs, and other creatures that appear when it rains. By painting rain-related designs on their water jars, Zuni potters show what the jars are for and, in a way, make a wish for enough water to keep the jars full.

Do the Zuni still make their own pottery today?

Yes, they do. Zuni potters make pots, jars, and bowls. However, it is more common for Zuni people to use metal and plastic pots and pans. Clay pots are also made for sale to tourists and collectors.

Do Zuni men and women both make pottery?

Traditionally, only women gathered clay and made pots, but men have always painted the designs onto them. Today both men and women are potters. Randy Nahohai, a contemporary Zuni potter whom we will meet on page 28, makes pots for ceremonial use and for sale.

the story of the foster child of the deer

Based on Frank Hamilton Cushing's
version of a Zuni folk tale, 1901

Deer were not only an important source of food for pueblo people, but, as this story will reveal, were also highly respected by the Zuni. One legend says that deer were valuable because they led humans to water, the desert's most precious resource.

One morning, long, long ago, in the mesas of the Southwest, at a place called Háwikuh, daylight was breaking. The hills and valleys emerged one after another from the shadows of the night. As a deer and her two brightly speckled little fawns stood drinking at a stream, they were startled by an infant's cry. Looking up, they saw dust and cotton wool and other things flying about in the air, as if blown by a whirlwind. The child—waking and finding itself alone, hungry, and cold—was crying and throwing its little hands about.

"What joy!" cried the deer to her fawns. "I have found a child, and though it is human it shall be mine, for you see, my children, I love you so much that surely I could love another." She breathed her warm breath upon him, caressed him, and carried him home on her broad horns. The Deer-mother was surprised and delighted to find that her little foster child grew even more swiftly than her own children. On the evening of the fourth day she was amazed to see that he was running about and playing with his foster brother and sister. And on the eighth day he had grown into a fair youth—strong, swifter of foot than the deer themselves, and quick to learn their language and their ways. So wise and strong was the youth that he soon became the leader of the deer, and much they loved him.

When the deer were out on the mesas ranging to and fro, the swift youth always ran at their head. The soles of his feet became as hard as the hoofs of the deer, the skin of his body strong and dark, and the hair of his head long and waving and as soft as the hair of the deer themselves.

This bowl, created by the Sikyathi, an earlier Southwest tribe, depicts a hunter and his prey, a deer.

But it chanced one morning, late that summer, that a hunter made his way toward the lair of the Deer-mother. As he crossed the borders of the great mesas that lay beyond, he saw a vast herd of deer gathered, as people gather in council. The hunter stole carefully along on his hands and knees, twisting himself among the bushes until he came near. Great was his wonder when he beheld in the midst of the deer a splendid youth—broad of shoulder and tall and strong of limb, sitting nude and graceful on the ground—with all of the deer, old and young, paying attention to what he was saying.

The hunter rubbed his eyes and looked again, but when he lifted himself to look more closely, the sharp eyes of the youth discovered him. With a shout, the youth lifted himself to his feet and sped away like the wind, followed by the whole herd, their hoofs thundering. Soon they were all out of sight.

When the deer had gone a safe distance, they slackened their pace and called to their leader not to fear. Then his old foster mother for the first time related to him that he was the child of mortals and told him how she had found him.

The youth sat with his head bowed, thinking of these things. Then he raised his head proudly, and said, "Though I be a child of mortals, they have not loved me; they have cast me from their midst. Therefore I will be faithful to you alone."

But the old Deer-mother said to him, "Hush, my child! You are but a mortal and though you can live on the roots of the trees and the bushes in summer and autumn, you will not be able to survive in the winter, when the fruits and nuts will all be gone."

The older members of the herd who had gathered round confirmed what she had said. And they went on, "We know that now we shall be hunted, as is always the custom when our herd has been discovered, on the fourth day from when we were first seen. Among the people who come there will

be, no doubt, those who will seek you. You must not endeavor to escape. You must return to your people and teach them to be brave hunters, sacred of thought and sacred of heart. You must teach them to make sacrifices to us, so that after we die, our new lives will be spared unceasing cruelty."

A splendid deer rose from the midst of the herd and, coming forward, laid his cheek on the cheek of the boy, and said, "Though we love you, we must now part from you." To all this the youth, being convinced, agreed.

Just as the herd had anticipated, four days later the hunters came. From the north and the west and the south and the east came an alarm. The deer began to scatter and then to assemble and scatter again. At last the hunters with drawn bows came running in, and soon their arrows were flying, and deer after deer fell.

At last but a few were left, among them the kind old Deer-mother and her two children. With the glorious youth at their lead, they ran and ran, the fleetest of the tribe pursuing them. The youth's foster brother was soon slain, and so, too, his foster sister. But the youth kept on, his old mother alone running behind him. Finally the hunters overtook the old mother, but when they caught her, they turned away, saying, "Faithful to the last has she been to this youth." Then they renewed the chase for the youth, who faced about and stood like a stag at bay. When they approached, he dropped his arms and lowered his head.

So was the foster child of the deer restored to his people. Because the youth had lived so long with the deer and had become acquainted with their every way and every word, he taught all of his children and all of his friends how to show respect for the deer. This happened in the days of the ancients, and to this day, because of him, there are sacred hunters of our tribe who understand the ways and language of the deer.

crack the zuni design code

Zuni pottery designs are not only beautiful but many are like secret codes, carrying special meaning for the Zuni people. Sometimes there is something easy to recognize, like an animal. Sometimes a design seems familiar, but it's hard to see what it represents at first. And sometimes the designs are just shapes, but they usually mean something special, like a wish or a prayer drawn in code.

This design was a baby ornament used to bring good luck in childhood.

This design shows feather clouds. Clouds mean rain, and rain means food.

The thin lines in this design are called "hatching." They represent falling rain. The black squares represent ears of corn. This symbol is sometimes used so that crops may be plentiful.

This is called "the deer in his house," and it is one of the most common designs on Zuni pots. One potter said that she painted the deer so that her husband would have success while hunting.

The line from the deer's mouth to its heart is called a "spirit line" or a "heartline." Some people have said that it shows the life or spirit of the animal. Some believed that if you could see inside an animal, you could control its spirit, and that the line is like a prayer to that spirit. The line is usually red and surrounded by a white space.

The swirling circular shapes, called the "rainbird motif," refer to the rain-bearing cumulus clouds as they roll in to the Zuni valley.

Now you be the detective

Each of these designs and symbols can be found on the water jars we have been looking at. See if you can find them.

patterns, and symbols

Animals in Zuni Art

The Zuni, like other Native Americans, have always lived and worked close to nature. They have watched the earth and its creatures closely to understand the cycles of the seasons and to help them in growing and hunting for food. While some native cultures give special meaning to particular animals, the Zuni have rarely been that specific. Although they do revere animals for their special skills, the Zuni mostly see them as creatures who share our planet and should be respected.

This bowl looks very different from the water jars we have been looking at. What differences do you see? How is the shape different? Would this bowl be helpful for carrying, pouring, or keeping things shaded and protected?

Since this bowl was for medicine water, someone needed to sprinkle things into it. How could you tell by the shape? In fact, the inside of the bowl is worn and stained, which probably means it was used for mixing special medicinal ingredients.

Look at the top edge of the bowl. The steplike shapes sticking out of the top are called "cloud terraces"; sometimes they represent clouds, sometimes mountains, and sometimes mesas. The painted symbols on the inside of the bowl are images that the Zuni associate with fertility: tadpoles, dragonflies, frogs, and a serpent with a feathered topknot, all of whom appear in Zuni myth. Notice that, like the deer in his house, the snake also has a spirit line.

Think about things that are extremely special to you. What are they? Do you treat them differently than ordinary things? Are they fancy or simple?

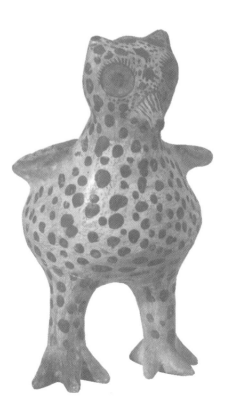

The Zuni admire the owl as a fierce and able hunter.

Some Zuni pottery was used every day, but other pieces were used only for special religious ceremonies. This bowl was used for "medicine water."

keeping the tradition alive

Randy Nahohai firing pots

Inspiration is drawn from everything, as we are surrounded by art: our mythology, religion and culture, as well as visual arts and, of course, natural beauty. In Zuni you can't help but be inspired by everything you see. . . . Most traditional pottery was made for a certain function, not for commercialization. Traditional Zuni pieces, in my opinion, exist only at Zuni, where they are used in daily life as well as for religious purposes.

Randy Nahohai

Randy Nahohai

learned the art of pottery from his mother, Josephine, who has been active in reintroducing traditional methods of Zuni pottery making. Randy and other members of his family often work together to create pots. Randy, who was born in 1957, likes to combine traditional and modern techniques to make pottery. He exhibits his work in museums and galleries throughout the United States.

How does Randy Nahohai help keep the Zuni pottery tradition alive?

Look at the Zuni water jars again and compare them to Randy Nahohai's pottery on this page. Compare shape and designs. Can you find a heartline? hatching (rain)? a rainbird? What's old about this pot? What's new about it? Randy Nahohai continues the Zuni pottery tradition, yet he also adapts it.

This jar was made by Randy Nahohai.

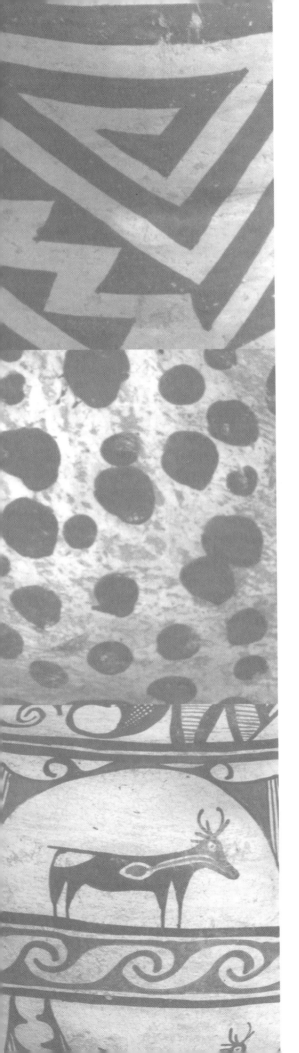

doing it for yourself

design a logo

People say a picture is worth a thousand words. Think about what designs you could create for yourself as a personal logo or to represent a club or your favorite sports team. If you're speedy, how about a lightning bolt? Are you the strong, silent type? Maybe a tree is more your style. Your design doesn't have to show something other people can recognize—you could start with an image from the real world and then change or simplify it, as Zuni potters did. Think about where you would put your design. On your book bag or binder? Perhaps the door to your room?

pottery without the wheel

Did you ever see pictures of people making pots, leaning over spinning wheels with blobs of clay on them? Zuni potters know another way to make a bowl, jar or cup, which you can try at home with clay or even Play-Doh.

Grab a handful of clay and start to roll it under both your palms against a flat surface until it looks like a long, skinny tube about a foot or so long. Make six or seven of these. When you're done, take one and coil it around in a tight, flat spiral shape. As you add each piece, pinch it together with the last one and keep coiling the clay around and around in an upward spiral as you build up the sides of your cup or bowl. When you have reached the top, take a flat stone or a Popsicle stick to smooth out the ridges between the coils.

Before you start, think about what shape you want to make. A bowl? A cup? A jar? A vase? What would you keep in it? If you like, you can paint a design on the surface of your pot. Or, you can carve a design into the side with a toothpick or a pencil tip.

Dowry Basket (Made by Jenny; Pomo)

This basket is 13¾ inches high and 27 inches in diameter. It is lattice-twined and made out of willow, sedge root, redbud, clamshell beads, glass beads, and cotton string. The Brooklyn Museum purchased the basket in 1907.

pomo

looking at a pomo basket

picture the size of the basket

from the measurements on the opposite page. What could you keep in a basket this size?

What objects have been used as cradles, trays, jars, bowls, nets, sacks, and mats for more than 10,000 years?

Baskets! This basket was given as a wedding present to a young Pomo couple starting their life together in a northern California river valley.

look at the design

How many colors did the basket maker use? What kinds of shapes did she use? How many different patterns do you see running around the sides of the basket? Do you see any places where the patterns are disrupted or changed?

Can you see anything that has been woven onto the surface of the basket? What is it?

look at the weave

Is it tight or loose? How did the weaver combine light and dark colors in one basket? (Is the color just on the surface or is it on the inside as well?) How long do you think it would take to create a basket like this?

a pomo basket weaver *at work*

Pomo woman gathering grasses

[Gathering grasses] can be either an adventure and lots of fun or drudgery and hard work depending on how you look at it.

Elsie Allen, Pomo Indian basket maker

Basket materials must be gathered at the proper time of year, when roots and new shoots are of the right length and thickness. Basket makers prefer sedge for a light, buff background, and bulrush and redbud for darker parts of the design.

Pomo baskets are mostly made of willow shoots. Weavers either use willow roots or sedge grass roots to make the white stitches. Bulrush roots make the black design. Redbud makes the reddish brown design.

Basket making is a time-consuming and painstaking process requiring much concentration and dexterity.

①
After collecting each material for basket making, the weaver prepares them for the traditional curing of one year. She splits and bundles them so they dry properly. The original tool was an obsidian blade, but today a knife is used.

②
The weaver plans a design. The same design may mean entirely different things to different weavers.

③
Next she weaves her basket. She keeps her materials pliable by soaking them in a container of water. She can twine or coil the materials depending on the intended use of the basket. Twining is used for more utilitarian baskets, such as those used for cooking, eating, storage, gathering, and transporting. Coiling is used for ceremonial, gift, or treasure baskets.

questions and answers about pomo culture

Where do the Pomo live?

The Pomo are not one tribe, but more than seventy groups loosely connected by language and culture. They live in northern California, among the lakes and valleys between the Russian and Sacramento rivers. They traditionally lived by hunting, fishing, and gathering. Acorns were a popular food.

The rivers and lakes of northern California provided fish to eat and plenty of plant materials for basketmaking.

How are Pomo baskets used?

Pomo baskets are used for everyday activities like cooking (after they have been soaked for protection), holding and serving food, playing games, and even carrying babies. Some baskets are made as gifts for special events like weddings or tribal ceremonies.

With their beautiful shapes, striking designs, and tight weave, Pomo baskets have long been admired by Indians and non-Indians alike.

Can a basket hold water?

Yes, it can. Pomo baskets are famous for their tight weave and have often been used to hold water.

Who makes baskets?

Traditionally both men and women made baskets. Men were responsible for making hunting traps, fishing weirs (traps), and baby baskets. Women made coiled and finely twined baskets.

How long does it take to make a basket?

It takes from a few months to several years, depending on the size, weave, and design.

Is this tradition still practiced today?

Yes, it is. There are Pomo basket makers who make baskets for everyday use. However, it is also common for Pomo Indians to use modern containers, made from plastic or metal, instead of baskets.

Who makes baskets today?

Many Native American tribes continue to weave baskets today. However, the Pomo Indians are famous for their fine useful basketry. Susan Billy, featured on page 40, is a Pomo Indian who currently weaves baskets.

Boat shaped basket made with abalone shell, bead ornaments, and feathers.

the story of the basket of plenty

Adapted from a Pomo myth as told by Cora Clark and her sister, Texa Bowen Williams

Long ago there lived a maiden called Baculbotet. She lived in a palace, for she was a very great lady with many servants to wait upon her. Her room was at the top of a wide stone stairway. She always lay upon her bed and was never seen outside her home.

People worshiped Baculbotet, and because her pure and innocent spirit dwelt in their hearts, they lived righteous lives. Sin and evil were unknown. People did not need to work, for Baculbotet was the Grain Maiden who provided them with all they needed.

But there came a time when the hunters were unable to find deer, and famine was in the land. Then Baculbotet rose from her bed, took her basket, and walked down the wide stairway.

Her parents and friends were astonished and asked why she had left her room. She turned to them and asked, "Why can the hunters kill no deer? Why have the people no food? I go to the river because I wish to go." She went down to a stream that flowed broad and deep before her home.

When she came to the bank of the river, she saw Weebchillen, the fearsome dragon, lying in the water. She said to him in a low, calm voice, "Ever since the world began, you have been a thing of evil. I know what you are, and I shall overcome you." Then she returned to her room, but told no one what she had seen.

Baculbotet left her room again the next day and walked down the wide stone stairway. This time she went to a wooded hillside, where she gathered materials for a basket. Into the basket she wove many designs that the people had never seen before. Strangely, the designs kept changing. Stranger still was the effect the basket had on the supply of food. As soon as the basket was finished, deer and other foods again became plentiful. Whenever any member of the tribe became hungry, all he or she had to do was reach into the basket of plenty. Even when visitors came and a bountiful feast was needed, Baculbotet would take out all that was needed, and still the basket remained full.

But Baculbotet knew that even though the power of her basket was stronger than that of Weebchillen, the food supply would be uncertain as long as he lived. As long as he remained on earth, no one would be safe. Therefore, she decided to destroy him.

In the morning she went out in search of the monster. Since she could not find him, she knew he was hiding in some dark pool, waiting to reappear and work his evil spell. Baculbotet pulled a long hair from her head. Making a loop in it, she firmly anchored it to a stake driven into the riverbank. She returned to her room, and all that night she sang her magic-working songs.

The next morning Baculbotet took her basket and walked down to the river's edge to see the result of her work. There was Weebchillen, securely held by the loop of hair. Now came the time to slay him with her magic powers. Weebchillen felt her power and feared it. With the loop of hair still about his neck, he swam to the head of the river. There he lay silent and helpless, weakened by her magic.

As he lay there, he changed the patterns on his back, hoping in this way to avoid the power of her incantations. However, each change on his back caused a similar change in the patterns on the basket.

In a low, calm voice, Baculbotet said to the evil dragon, "You gained control of the food, but now the control has passed from you to this basket." And she placed it in front of him.

Weebchillen seemed to give up. He lay there as if lifeless, so the brave maiden thought he was dead. Baculbotet returned to her people, who were already feasting in celebration of his defeat. But the wily old dragon had only pretended to be dead. Suddenly the fearsome beast appeared among the feasters and crushed Baculbotet with his lashing tail.

Her friends rushed to her, but it was too late. Where she had fallen, there lay not a lovely maiden, but a fawn of spotless white, which got to its feet and bounded away into the forest.

Since the death of Baculbotet, the White Fawn Maiden, evil has come into the hearts of men, and they have been forced to search for food with much difficulty. This has brought greed, dishonesty, unkindness, and wars without number into the world.

Today, the White Fawn is still sometimes seen. But only a few have caught glimpses of her, for she is only visible to those who are pure of heart.

thinking about pomo baskets

Sometimes for a special basket, very small feathers are woven onto the outside surface as the basket is being made. The weaver might also add clamshell beads and abalone pieces, using string made from Indian hemp.

baskets for special occasions

In many cultures around the world, when a couple gets married, the bride's parents give the groom a gift or series of gifts called a dowry. The basket on page 32 is called a dowry basket. Dowry baskets are among the largest of Pomo baskets. Why do you think that is?

What clues do you have that this basket was made for a special occasion? Look at its condition. Does it look used? Look at the size and the tightness of the weave. Do you think it took a long time to make? Does it have any special decorative elements?

Look at the basket pictured to the left. It, too, was used for a special purpose. How can you tell? How many different types of decoration can you find?

What gifts have you received on special occasions in your life? What do they look like? Do they have any special decoration? Do they remind you of the spirit or feeling of that occasion? How? How do you take care of these things?

what's wrong with this picture?

If you look closely at Pomo baskets, you'll see that most are decorated with horizontal bands interrupted by a break or change in their design. Can you find such a break on the dowry basket?

You may think that these breaks in the design are mistakes. Actually, the weaver makes them on purpose.

An intentional change in the design pattern is called a door or "dau." This comes from an ancient Pomo myth. The tale recalls how the spirits who inhabit baskets came to the great coyote spirit after he had finished making the world and people and asked him for a village or a home to be theirs always. He responded by giving them the dau, saying "the door of the basket will always keep swinging for you to escape through when you die. Then you will ascend to the upper sky to live forever, where there is no sickness, where it is always day, where all are happy."

Here's another Pomo basket.
Can you find the dau?

39

keeping the tradition alive

Susan Billy, applying the final row to a basket

I was blessed to spend sixteen years learning from my great-aunt Elsie Allen. In the beginning, I literally sat at her feet for the first five years, studying with her every day. As I began to learn about basket weaving, I realized it couldn't be separated from the traditions and customs, the religion, the taboos — the whole way of living. To me, these traditional beliefs have a power of their own, something I can't fully understand, yet this gives me a link to my ancestors.

On my first day of weaving, as I walked into the room, my great-aunt held out her hand and gave me an old awl and knife. She said, "These were your grandmother's and I want you to have them. They are yours now." At that magic moment, my grandmother's spirit was passed on to me. . . . I feel her smiling on me and her spirit with me when I'm weaving.

Susan Billy

Susan Billy

learned the art of Pomo basket weaving from her great-aunt Elsie Allen, one of the foremost Pomo weavers. Born in 1951, Susan Billy now lives in Ukiah, California, where she owns a shop selling her beaded jewelry. She also exhibits her basketry around the country.

How does Susan Billy keep Pomo traditions alive?
Look at the dowry basket on page 32 and Susan Billy's basket on this page. Compare shape, designs, and special decorations. How are they similar? How are they different? Can you find any places where she might have left an opening or break in the design for the spirits to escape?

Is there anything special you have learned from your parents or grandparents or other members of your families? Have they shared any special skills with you? Family recipes? Cultural traditions?

Susan Billy made this tiny basket.

doing it for yourself

be a basket detective

Baskets are all around us. You can probably find several right in your own home any time of year. They can be plain or fancy, large or small, useful or just decorative.

Go around your home and make a list of all the baskets you find. (Look on shelves, in the kitchen, on dressers, and around house plants.) Which is the largest? Which is the smallest? What are they used for? Notice whether they have designs on the surface and whether those designs are painted or created by weaving different colored materials. Look at the weave of each basket. Is it tight or loose? Do you think any could hold water like some Pomo baskets? Are any other materials woven into them, like ribbons or feathers? Do you know where any of them came from or who made them?

Pomo basketry materials: natural and processed willow root, sedge root, bulrush root, and redbud stems

weave your own basket

Materials

1. Four posterboard strips, each measuring 12 inches long by 1 inch wide. If you like, use a ruler to trace the shape. You can use strips of one color, or you can mix them for a more colorful basket.

2. Scissors

3. Hole punch

4. Paper fasteners

5. Colored yarn, string, or ribbons, no shorter than 12 inches long

6. Beads, buttons, feathers, or other decorative objects

Instructions

1. Cut out the four posterboard strips and, using the hole punch, make a hole in the center of each strip. Lay them on top of one another. Attach them all together in the center by inserting a paper fastener through all four holes. Once they are securely fastened, fan the strips out at different angles so that they look like spokes in a wheel.

2. You will need an odd number of spokes in order to weave properly. So, after they are attached, cut off one spoke just above where it is fastened. You should have seven spokes.

3. With your string or yarn or ribbon, you will make the basket take its shape. Make sure that whatever material you use is long enough to go around your spokes at least once, with extra to spare. Leave a few inches of posterboard strip on each side of the center fastener at the bottom for a base, then begin to weave the yarn around the spokes, over and under, over and under, spiraling upward as you go. Decide if you want to make a pattern by alternating your weaving

materials. When one material runs out, you can end it with a knot on the inside of the basket, or you can tie it to the next piece you will be using. If you are using a pattern, think about how you could create a *dau*, or break in your pattern, as Pomo weavers do.

4. As you spiral upward, pull the yarn gently so the spokes become vertical. Be careful not to pull the yarn too tightly.

5. Attach beads, buttons, feathers, or other objects to your baskets as you go along. You can look at the dowry basket for inspiration.

6. When you get to the top, you can fold the top edges down and weave them securely into the basket for a finished look, or you can cut them to make a more open, decorative look (like the top of a picket fence).

exploring museums on your own

Think back to the careful looking you have done. We have looked at Native American artworks by exploring patterns, function, form, design, texture, symbols, stories, materials, and processes used to make the object. Thinking about these things will help when you are looking at art from any culture. The works of art in a museum are sometimes very rare, or delicate, or valuable, which is why these objects are protected by museums for all of us to see. But when you go to a museum you can "collect" your own objects by writing about them, drawing them, or buying postcards of them in the museum shop.

Here are some tips on how to make a collection of your own favorite works of art.

1. Visit a museum or a Native American cultural center near you. (Look at the list on page 46 for some suggestions of places to go.) Take some paper or a pad and a pencil with you.

2. Look for masks, pottery, or baskets from any culture. Look carefully at the patterns, shapes, and symbols on the works of art you like best.

3. Draw each object you like and write down why you chose it. Does it remind you of something familiar? Note what materials were used to make it, what colors you see. How would it feel if you could touch it? Does it have a pattern? Are there symbols in the pattern? How do you think it was used? Who used it?

4. Once you've found two or three more objects and have thought about the questions above, you can get started on your own museum memories at home. In addition to your drawings, you might want to buy museum postcards of your objects or take photos of the artworks you choose (*ask a guard if it's okay to take pictures*).

5. Once you are home, find some cardboard or paper big enough to make a poster. Decide how you want to space the objects on your poster. Draw the objects and color them in with paints, crayons, or colored pencils. You might want to use glue to combine your drawings with some of the postcards you bought at the museum, or cut up a brochure you got while you were there. This technique is called collage.

6. Hang the poster in your room and share your art memories with family and friends.

7. If you do not want to draw the objects, you may want to write about what they look like, tell a story about them, or tell a friend about your experience at the museum. You might even want to keep a special notebook or journal that you use only when you visit museums.

recommended books on native american indian art and culture

for adults

Allen, Elsie. *Pomo Basketmaking: A Supreme Art for the Weaver*. Healdsburg, California: Nature Graph Publishers, 1972.

Barrett, S.A. *Pomo Myths*. Milwaukee, Wisconsin: Cannon Printing Company, 1933.

——. *Basket Designs of the Pomo Indians*. Berkeley, California: California Indian Library Collections, 1992.

Boas, Franz. *Kwakiutl Tales, Columbia University Contributions to Anthropology*, vol. 2. New York: Columbia University Press, 1910.

Bunzel, Ruth L. *The Pueblo Potter: A Study of Creative Imagination in Primitive Art*. New York: Dover Publications, 1972.

Coe, Ralph T. *Lost and Found Traditions: Native American Art 1965-1985*. New York: The American Federation of Arts, 1986.

——. *Sacred Circles, Two Thousand Years of North American Indian Art*. London: Arts Council of Great Britain, 1976.

Culin, Stewart. *Games of the North American Indians*. Lincoln, Nebraska: University of Nebraska, 1992.

Dittert, A.E., Jr., and F. Plog. *Generations in Clay: Pueblo Pottery of the American Southwest*. Flagstaff, Arizona: Northland Press, in cooperation with The American Federation of Arts, 1980.

Eagle, Walking Turtle. *Indian America, A Traveler's Companion*. Santa Fe, New Mexico: John Muir Publications, 1989.

Erdoes, R. and A. Ortiz, eds. *American Indian Myths and Legends*. New York: Pantheon, 1984.

Fane, Diana, Ira Jacknis, and Lise B. Breen. *Objects of Myth and Memory: American Indian Art at The Brooklyn Museum*. Brooklyn, New York and Seattle, Washington: The Brooklyn Museum and the University of Washington Press, 1991.

Gattuso, John, ed. *Native America. Insight Guides*. Singapore: APA Publications, 1991.

Harvey, Karen D., Lisa D. Harjo, and Jane K. Jackson. "Teaching about Native Americans," *Bulletin No. 84*. Washington, D.C.: National Council for the Social Studies, 1990.

Holm, Bill. *Northwest Coast Indian Art: An Analysis of Form*. Seattle, Washington: University of Washington Press, 1971.

Spirit and Ancestor: A Century of Northwest Coast Indian Art at the Burke Museum. Seattle, Washington: University of Washington Press, 1987.

James, George Wharton. *Indian Basketry*. New York: Dover Publications, 1972.

Jonatis, Aldona, ed. *Chiefly Feasts: The Enduring Kwakiutl Potlatch*. New York: American Museum of Natural History, 1991.

Macnair, Peter L. *The Legacy*. Vancouver, Canada: British Columbia Provincial Museum, 1984.

Nabokov, Peter, ed. *Native American Testimony: A Chronicle of Indian-White Relations from Prophecy to the Present, 1492-1992*. New York: Viking Penguin, 1992.

——. *Native Peoples: The Arts and Lifeways*. Phoenix, Arizona: Media Concepts Group.

Ortiz, Alfonso. *The Pueblo*. New York: Chelsea House Publishers, 1992.

Penney, David W. *Art of the American Indian Frontier: A Portfolio*. New York: The New Press and the Detroit Institute of Arts, 1995.

Rodee, Marian, and James Ostler. *Zuni Pottery*. Pennsylvania: Schiffer Publishing Ltd., 1986.

Stewart, Hilary. *Looking at Indian Art of the Northwest Coast*. Seattle, Washington: University of Washington Press, 1979.

Wade, Edwin L., ed. *The Arts of the North American Indians: Native Traditions in Evolution*. New York: Hudson Hills Press, 1986.

Waldman, C. *Atlas of North American Indians*. New York: Facts on File, 1985.

Walens, Stanley. *The Kwakiutl*. New York: Chelsea House Publishers, 1992.

Weatherford, Jack. *Indian Givers: How the Indians of the Americas Transformed the World*. New York: Crown Publishers, 1988.

Zuni People. *The Zunis*. Albuquerque, New Mexico: University of New Mexico Printing Plant, 1972.

for children

Amon, A. *The Earth is Sore: Native Americans on Nature*. New York: Atheneum, 1981.

Baylor, Byrd. *When Clay Sings*. New York: Macmillan Publishing Company, 1972.

Bruchac, Joseph. *Iroquois Stories: Heroes and Heroines, Monsters and Magic*. Freedom, California: Crossing Press, 1985.

——. *Return of the Sun: Native American Tales From the Northeast Woodlands*. Freedom, California: The Crossing Press.

Cohlene, Terri. *Quillworker: A Cheyenne Legend*. Mahwah, New Jersey: Watermill Press, 1990.

——. *Turquoise Boy: A Navajo Legend*. Mahwah, New Jersey: Watermill Press, 1990.

D'Alleva, Anne. *Native American Arts and Cultures*. Worcester, Massachusetts: Davis Publications, 1993.

Fox, Frank. *North American Indians*. Los Angeles: Troubador Press, 1987.

Gabel, Paul. *The Gift of the Sacred Dog*. New York: Macmillan Publishing Company, 1987.

——. *The Great Race of Birds and Animals*. New York: Macmillan Publishing Company, 1991.

Siberell, Anne. *Whale in the Sky*. New York: E.P. Dutton, 1982.

museums and native american cultural sites

Alaska Native Village
Alaskaland Park
Fairbanks, AK 99701
(907) 459-1087

Anchorage Museum
of History and Art
121 W. 7th Avenue
Anchorage, AK 99501
(907) 343-4326

Totem Heritage Center
601 Deermont
Ketchikan, AK 99901

Southeast Alaska
Indian Cultural Center
106 Metlakatla
Sitka, AK 99835
(907) 747-8061

Arizona State Museum
University of Arizona
Tucson, AZ 85721
(602) 621-6281

Gila River Arts and
Crafts Center
P.O. Box 457
Sacaton, AZ 85247
(602) 963-3981

The Heard Museum
22 East Monte Vista Road
Phoenix, AZ 85004
(602) 252-8848

Hopi Tribal Museum
P.O. Box 7, Highway 264
Second Mesa, AZ 86043
(602) 734-6650

Museum of North Arizona
Route 4, P.O. Box 720
Flagstaff, AZ 86001
(602) 774-5211

Chaw-se Regional
Indian Museum
Indian Grinding Rocks
State Park
14881 Pine Grove—Volcano Road
Pine Grove, CA 95665

Robert H. Lowie
Museum of Anthropology
103 Kroeber Hall
University of California
Berkeley, CA 94720
(510) 642-3681

Southwest Museum
P.O. Box 41558
Los Angeles, CA 90042
(213) 221-2163

Denver Art Museum
100 West 14th Avenue Parkway
Denver, CO 80204
(303) 640-2295

Tantaquidgeon Indian Museum
1819 N. New London Road
Uncasville, CT 06382
(203) 848-9145

Miccosukee Cultural Center
P.O. Box 440021
Miami, FL 33144
(305) 223-8380

The Art Institute of Chicago
Michigan Avenue
at Adams Street
Chicago, IL 60603
(312) 443-3914

Field Museum
of Natural History
Roosevelt Road at Lake
Shore Drive
Chicago, IL 60605
(312) 922-9410

Wampanoag Indian Program
of Plymouth Plantation
137 Warren Avenue
Plymouth, MA 02360
(508) 746-1622

Museum of the Plains Indian
and Craft Center
P.O. Box 400
Browning, MT 59417
(406) 338-2230

Museum of the Cherokee Indian
P.O. Box 1599,
U.S. Highway 441 North
Cherokee, NC 28719
(704) 497-3481

Indian Pueblo
Cultural Center, Inc.
2401 12th Street, NW
Albuquerque, NM 87104
(505) 242-4943

Institute of American Indian
Arts Museum
1018 Cathedral Place
Santa Fe, NM 87501
(505) 988-6281

Red Rock Museum
P.O. Box 328
Church Rock, NM 87311
(505) 863-1337

The Wheelright Museum of the
American Indian
704 Camino Lejo
Santa Fe, NM
(505) 982-4636

The Brooklyn Museum
200 Eastern Parkway
Brooklyn, NY 11238
(718) 638-5000

American Indian
Community House
404 Lafayette Street
Second Floor
New York, NY 10003
(212) 598-0100

American Museum of Natural
History
79th Street and Central
Park West
New York, NY 10024
(212) 769-5000

Akwesasne Museum
Route 37
St. Regis Mohawk Reservation
Hogansburg, NY 13655
(518) 358-2240

National Museum
of the American Indian
Smithsonian Institution
1 Bowling Green
New York, NY
(212) 668-6624

Native American Center
for the Living Arts, Inc.
25 Rainbow Blvd. South
Niagara Falls, NY 14303
(716) 284-2427

Cherokee National Museum
Cherokee Heritage Center
P.O. Box 515
Tahlequah, OK 74465
(918) 456-6007

Five Civilized Tribes Museum
Honor Heights Drive
Agency Hill
Muskogee, OK 74401
(918) 683-1701

Southern Plains Indian Museum
and Crafts Center
P.O. Box 749
Anadarko, OK 73005
(405) 247-6211

Tomaquag Indian Memorial
Museum
Summit Road
Exeter, RI 02822
(401) 539-7213

Sioux Indian Museum
and Craft Center
P.O. Box 1504
Rapid City, SD 57709
(605) 348-0557

Sacred Circle Gallery
of American Indian Art
P.O. Box 99100
Seattle, WA 98199
(206) 285-4425

Yakima Nation
Cultural Center Museum
P.O. Box 151
Toppenish, WA 98948
(509) 865-2800

Oneida Nation Museum
892 EE Road
DePere, WI 54115
(414) 869-2768

Information on objects seen in this book

Museums take great care keeping track of all the objects or works of art that they own. When you go to a museum you will find information on the label next to each object. Usually you can find out what a work of art is called, who made it, when it was made or purchased, what it is made of, how big it is, who gave it to the museum, and what year it came to the museum. The number at the bottom of each listing is called the accession number. This number helps the staff keep track of every single artwork in the museum. If you ever come to The Brooklyn Museum, you can look for these objects in the galleries because you have all the information you need to find them. Sometimes an object is not on view because it is being cleaned, or it has been borrowed by another museum, or someone might be studying it in another location. Remember, feel free to ask a guard or someone at an information desk for help if you are having trouble finding something.

Most of the objects shown in this book were purchased for The Brooklyn Museum by Stewart Culin, who was a curator at the Museum in the early 1900s. The location and date refer to Stewart Culin's expeditions to California, the Southwest, and the Northwest Coast. Culin also made careful notes about what materials each object was made of in his expedition reports. When you see a word with a question mark after it, that means we are not sure if the information is absolutely correct. The size of each object is listed in inches as H. (Height); D. (Depth); Diam. (Diameter); and W. (Width).

	Whale Mask Tenaxtax, Kwakiutl	Cedar wood, hide, cotton cord, leather, nails, pigment, H. 24, L. 68, W. 28 1/4	Collected by C. F. Newcombe in Knight Inlet, British Columbia; purchased in Victoria, July 15, 1908 08.491.8901
	Thunderbird Transformation Mask Nimpkish, Kwakiutl	Cedar wood, pigment, leather, nails, metal plate H. 17, L. 29 1/2, W. (closed) 12 1/2, W. (open) 71.	Collected by C. F. Newcombe in Alert Bay, British Columbia; purchased in Victoria, July 15, 1908 08.491.8902
	Carved and Painted Box Panel Kwakiutl?	Cedar wood, pigment, L. 12 3/4, W. 26 3/4, D. 1/2	Collected by C. F. Newcombe?; purchased in Victoria, British Columbia, August 13, 1905? 05.258
	Wolf Clan Helmet Haida?, Northwest Coast	Wood, paint, bone L. 17 3/4, D. 16 1/4	X378
	Water Jars Zuni	Ceramic, slip H. 11, D. 13 3/4; H. 12, D. 14 1/2	Purchased in Zuni, New Mexico, 1904 04.297.5248; 04.297.5249, Museum Collection Fund Photograph by Justin Kerr
	Paint Mortar with Pestles Zuni	Stone, traces of paint, H. 1 1/2, L. 12 1/4 (mortar); L. 8 1/2, 15 1/2 (pestles)	Purchased in Zuni, New Mexico, 1903 03.325.3459.1-.3
	Polishing Stones Zuni	Stone, L. 2 1/2, W. 2 1/4	Purchased in Zuni, New Mexico, 1903 03.325.3461.1-.7
	Bowl Sikyatki, 1400-1625	Ceramic, slip H. 3 3/4, D. 10 1/2	Given by Father Anselm Weber in Saint Michaels, Arizona, 1903 03.325.4328, Gift of Father Anselm Weber
	Owl Figure New Mexico, Zuni, late 19th century	Clay, paint H. 12 1/4, W. 7 1/2	X946
	Ceremonial Bowl Zuni	Ceramic, slip H. 8 1/2, D. 14 3/4	Purchased from Andrew Vanderwagen in Zuni, New Mexico, 1903 03.325.4721
	Dowry Basket Made by Jenny; Pomo	Twined: willow, sedge root, redbud bark, clamshell beads, glass beads, cotton string H. 13 3/4, Diam. 27	Purchased from Malpas and B. C. Cosgrove in Ukiah, California, July 12, 1907 07.467.8305
	Clamshell Pomo	Clamshell, L. 5 1/2, W. 3 3/4	Purchased from Joe Augustine in Lakeport, California, August 22, 1906 06.331.8011.1
	Clamshell Blanks for Beads Pomo	Clamshell, D. 3/4, D. 1/4	Purchased from Goose in Upper Lake, California, 1906 06.331.8160.1-.81
	Clamshell Beads Pomo	Clamshell, cotton string, L. 132, D. 3/4	Purchased in Upper Lake, California, August 16, 1906 06.331.7958

	Willow root (natural)	tied with cattail? W. 1 1/2, D. 5 1/4	Purchased from Nancy Graves in Upper Lake, California, August 5, 1907 07.467.8341.1 –.2
	Willow root (processed)	tied with cattail? W. 1, D. 3 1/2	Purchased from Nancy Graves in Upper Lake, California, August 5, 1907 07.467.8341.1 –.2
	Sedge root	L. 14 1/2, W. 4, D. 1 3/4	Purchased in Upper Lake, California, September 14, 1906 06.331.8131
	Bulrush root	tied with Indian hemp L. 14 3/4, Diam. 2 1/2	Purchased from Susana Graves in Upper Lake, California, August 31, 1906 06.331.8063
	Redbud stems	tied with Indian hemp? W. 1 1/2, D. 7	Purchased in Upper Lake, California, September 23, 1906 06.331.8146
	Boat-Shaped Basket Pomo, 19th century	Abalone shell and bead ornaments, feathers H. 3, D. 1/2	Gift of Mrs. Frederic B. Pratt 36.523
	Mush Basket (detail) Made by Elsie [Lake?] Pomo	Coiled: willow, sedge root, redbush bark H. 4 1/2, D. 9 1/4	Purchased from Elsie [Lake?] in Potter Valley, California, May 29, 1908 08.491.8639

These objects and photographs were generously loaned to us by the artists, and do not belong to The Brooklyn Museum:

- Susan Billy applying the final row to a basket, Hopland, California, 1977. Photograph by Ted Coe.

- Susan Billy (b. 1951). *Basket*, 1985. Sedge, redbud, single willow rod foundation,
  H. 1 3/4, W. 4 3/4. Collection of The American Federation of Arts.

- Richard Hunt.

- Randy Nahohai firing pottery in Zuni, New Mexico. Photograph by James Ostler.

- Randy Nahohai (b. 1957) *Olla (Jar)*, 1990 Clay, slip, Laboratory of Anthropology/Museum of Indian Arts
  and Culture, Santa Fe.

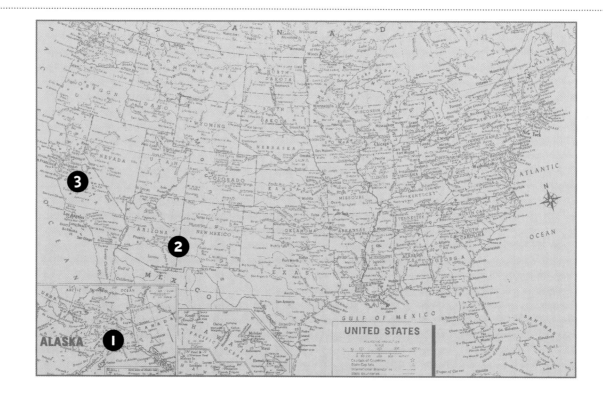

❶ **Kwakiutl Region**

❷ **Zuni Region**

❸ **Pomo Region**